Poo You and THE POTOROO'S LOO

by **DAVID BELLAMY**

illustrated by **Mic Rolph**

*Making***sense***of***science**

Children's Books

series editor **Fran Balkwill**

Portland Press

Making **sense** *of* **science**

Children's Books

Other titles in the series

BRAINBOX by **Steven Rose & Alexander Lichtenfels**

LIGHT UP YOUR LIFE by **David Phillips** • **PLANET OCEAN** by **Brian Bett**

SATELLITE FEVER by **Mike Painter** • **THE SPACE PLACE** by **Helen Sharman**

Author's acknowledgement:
To my grandson Theo

We wish to thank the following people who assisted in the production of this book:
Editorial Advisor SUSAN DICKINSON
For Portland Press SOPHIE CAYGILL and ADAM MARSHALL
THAMES WATER AUTHORITY
COMPASSION IN WORLD FARMING
DR VAL STANDEN
PROFESSOR DAVID WALKER

First published in 1997 by Portland Press Ltd
59 Portland Place, London W1N 3AJ, UK

ISBN 1 85578 095 X   ISSN 1355 8560

Typeset by Portland Press Ltd
Originated and printed by Cambridge University Press, Cambridge, UK

This book is about **poo**.

It may be yucky, it may be mucky, but it is fascinating and very important stuff. You make it every day from raw materials imported from around the world.

In your lifetime you will use at least 22 trees worth of toilet paper, just to keep you going!

You are an international poo factory, a prime poo-llutor of our planet!

Long before people arrived on the continent of Australia, the **potoroos** had solved the problem. Their recycling toilets at the base of gumtrees helped the trees to grow and kept the air fresh, with the smell of oil of eucalyptus.

The time has come for the world to learn
the lesson of the potoroo's loo.
Yeah!

There are many different names for poo. **Excreta** (ex-creet-ah) and **faeces** (fee-seas) are the proper scientific terms. Doctors and nurses often call them stools. This old-fashioned name comes from a low wooden stool with a hole in it that was set over a pit in the garden.

The courtiers at Hampton Court shared a multi-holer...

...while Good Queen Bess sat on a lone throne.

People who lived in towns were not so lucky. When the pits were full of poo, it had to be dug out and carted away. At night, for convenience, they emptied their chamber pots out of the window.

Hooray for Thomas Crapper! He used a cistern and chain to flush our poo problems down the drain.

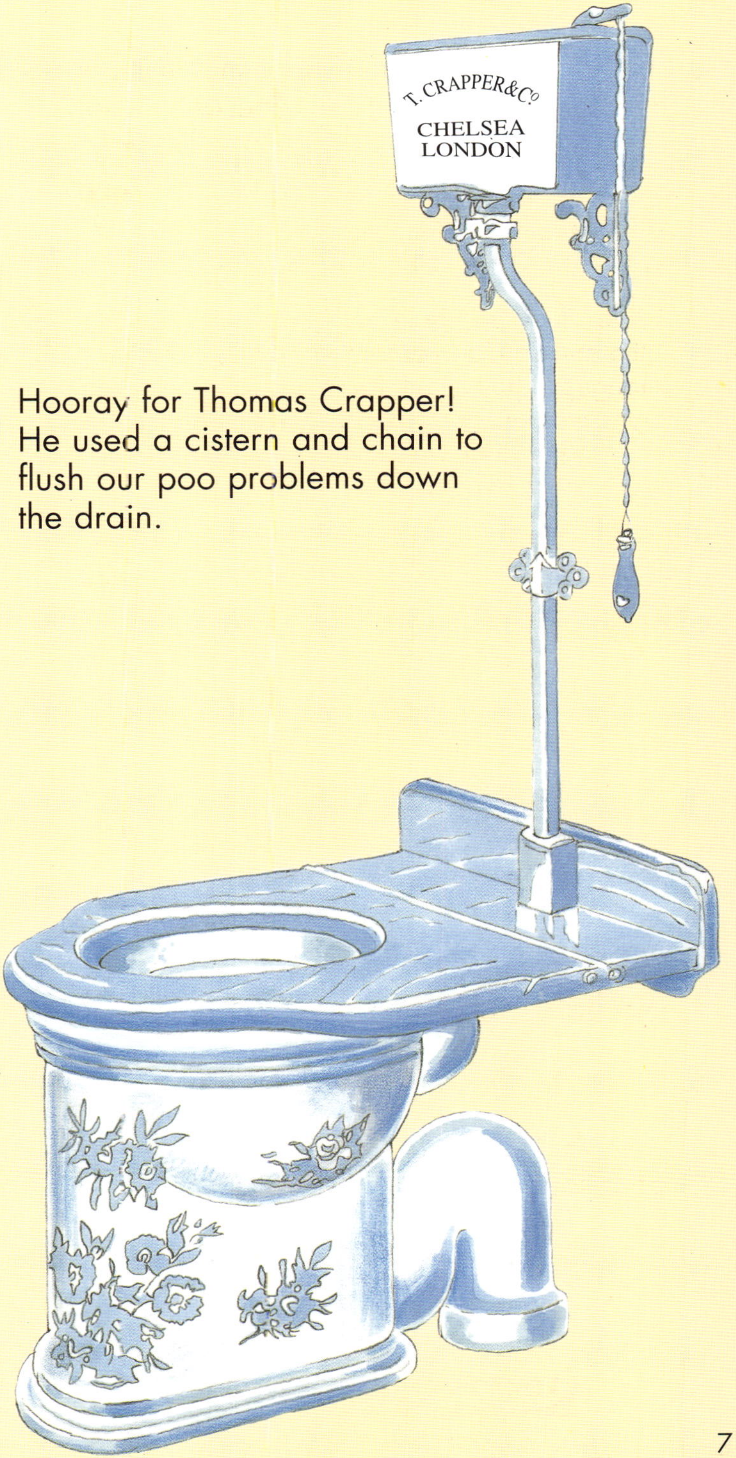

Whatever you call it, poo starts its life as food, glorious food. Each day you take in about 800 grams of solid and one and a half litres of liquid at the top, and plop out some 150 grams of wet poo at where else but the bottom! In between, there is a highly efficient food-processing plant – your **digestive system**.

Teeth slice and grind the food. Take a look in the mirror. Can you see two holes under your tongue? They are the exits from one of the three sets of chemical factories called **glands**. Together they secrete one and a half litres of **saliva** (sal-eye-va) every day.

Saliva helps make food slippery and contains **enzymes**. Enzymes are chemical crunchers that break down food to release energy-rich sugars just for you.

Swallowing throws the food down into the **oesophagus** (ee-sof-fag-us), a tube that's got rhythm! Waves of muscular contraction called **peristalsis** (perry-stal-sis) push the food on a one-way trip towards the stomach.

Your **stomach** is a muscular churn where the food is mixed with more enzymes and hydrochloric acid. All that churning and digesting creates gas, which mixes with the air you swallow to make big burps.

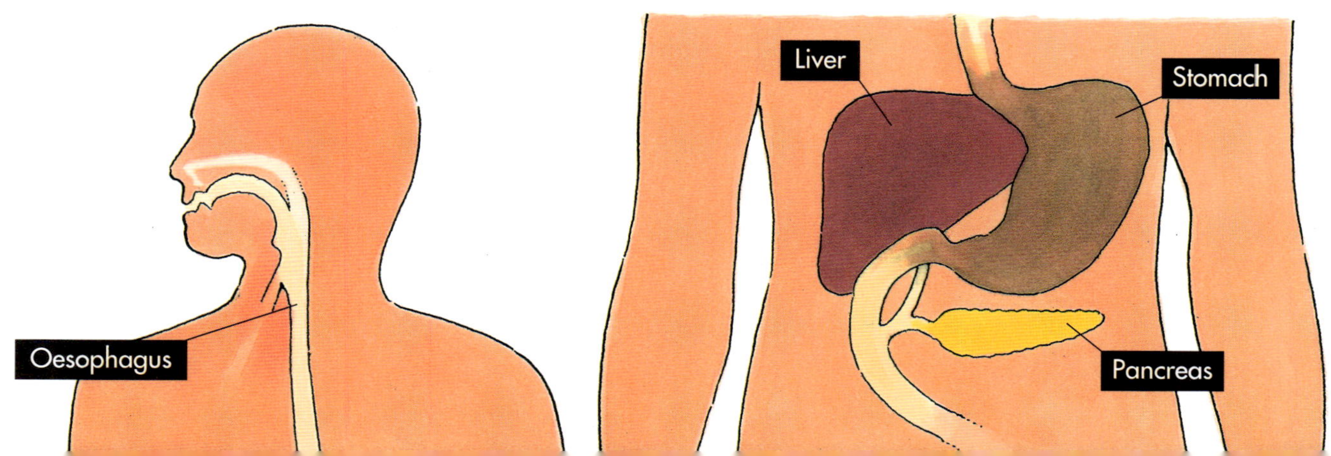

The chemical crunching is completed in the first 25 centimetres of your **small intestine**. This is helped by your **pancreas**, which neutralizes the acid, and your **liver,** which makes super-detergents to deal with fats.

What started as fish and chips is now sugars, fatty acids and amino acids, your own chemical building blocks. Over the next five and a half metres all these chemical goodies move into your bloodstream and are transported to where they are needed.

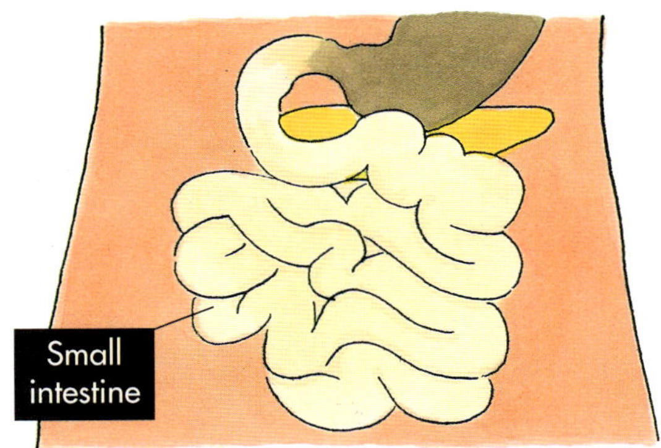

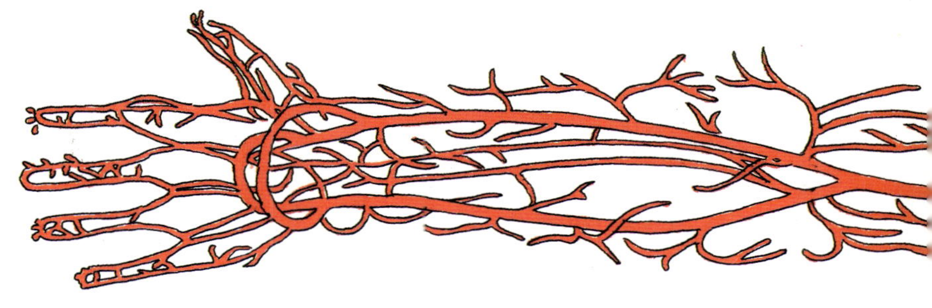

The leftovers pass to the **kidneys,** where they are turned into **urine** (wee). The **bowel** produces your poo. It reduces waste by recycling precious water. Billions of friendly bacteria feed on it, reducing its volume still further. They also make about half a litre of gas a day, which can pong a lot!

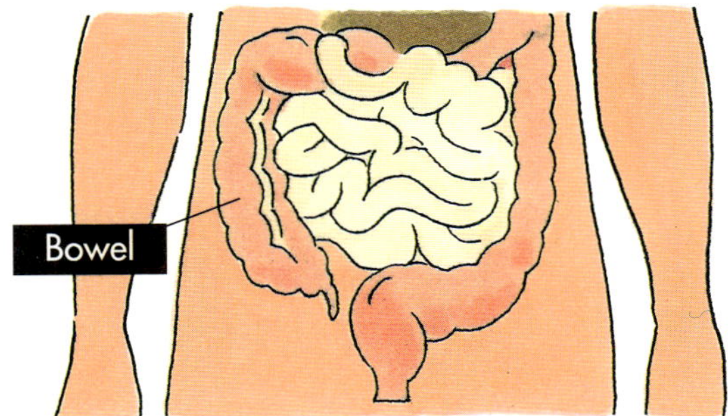

The food that cannot be digested plops out of the **rectum** through a valve called the **anus**. You can control this valve yourself, keeping it tight shut until you have to go.

And when you've got to go...
You've got to go !!

The waste that makes poo gives your gut muscles something to push against and keeps it all on the move. Always eat plenty of fruit and fibre to keep your gut and all those bacteria happy!

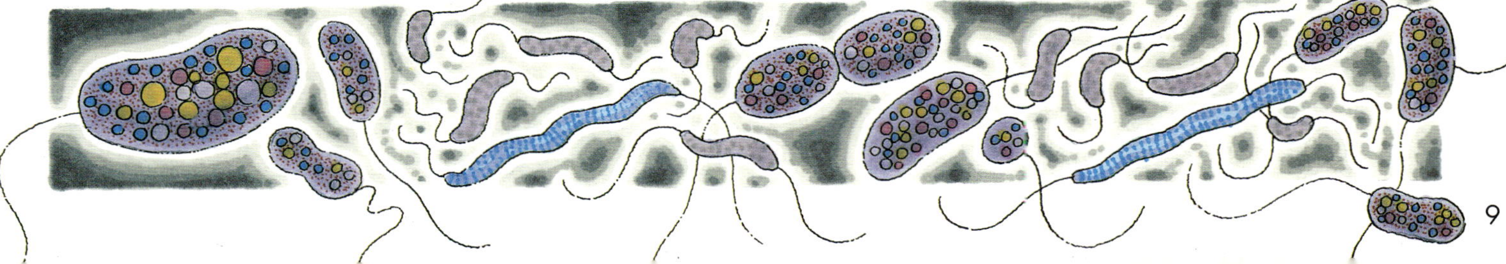

Bats hang upside down all day, fast asleep. They poo as they take off, covering lofts with high-grade fertilizer. Bats and all other mammals, except the pouch bearers and egg layers, poo and wee from separate exits. They have an anus and a **urethra** (you-reeth-rah).

Often the first signs that you are sharing your house with mice are tiny black poos in the most inconvenient places.

Cats are fastidious; they dig holes and cover their traces with soil.

Dog poo is really smelly and can contain **parasite** eggs, which can make humans ill. Dog loos and super pooper scoopers clean up the mess.

All other animals with skeletons pwoo, through a single opening called a **cloaca** (cloe-ache-ah). They pwoo while swimming, walking, perching and, unfortunately for us, flying.

Pigeons and starlings often roost in large numbers, especially in towns. The chemicals in their pwoo eat into stone and ironwork, causing great damage.

Turdus merula is the scientific name for the blackbird, who loves to eat worms.

There are worms at the bottom of your garden and they make very important poo from their tail ends. (They wee, wee, wee from special openings on every segment as they wiggle along.) Worms eat dead matter in the soil, cleaning it as they go. They till the soil, and the tunnels they make help air to get in and water to drain away. Some make spiral poos, called casts, on the surface.

For every large worm, there are thousands of smaller pot worms. All squiggling, eating and digesting, they poo pure organic **humus** (hew-mus), all that's left of dead plants and animals. Compost heaps are great places to discover worms. People now keep them in worm farms, where they speed composting.

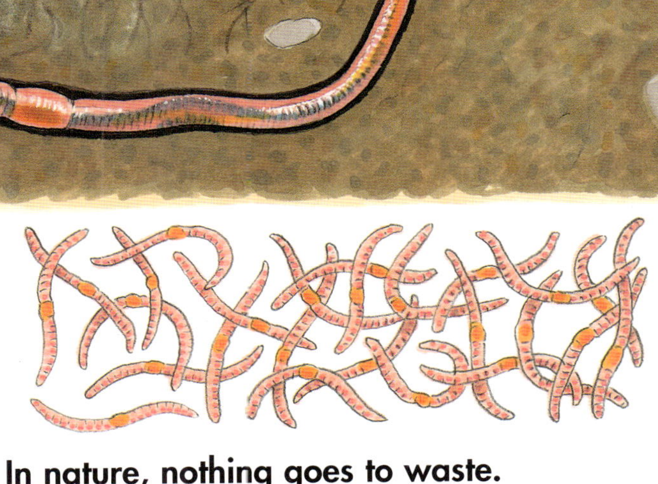

In nature, nothing goes to waste. Poo or pwoo is a precious resource.

At Perth Zoo in Australia you can buy poo in bags, all ready to plop on your garden.

Nearby New Zealand is the home of the takahe (tah-kah-hay). Thank goodness it can't fly because it makes eight metres of pwoo each day!

Honey Guides lead people to wild bee nests. They are the only birds that can digest beeswax, so their pwoo is unique. You could make candles out of Honey Guide pwoo!

Hippos wag their tails like very fast windscreen wipers, spreading the poo to stake out their chosen route from land to wallow and to show who is in charge.

Giraffes produce the world record long-drop product, which flattens on impact.

Rhinos are communal pooers, making piles over one metre high and seven metres wide.

Camels have humps to store energy for their life in dry deserts. Their fresh poo is so dry it is used to kindle camp fires!

Sloths live up trees but place their poo on the ground.

The world's fastest poo is made by the cheetah. This poo can travel at nearly 100 kilometres per hour (inside the animal of course).

Flamingoes keep themselves real cool by pwooing down their legs! The tops of their legs have lots of tiny blood vessels close to the surface. This means that they act as **heat exchangers**. Water in the pwoo evaporates, and cools the birds down.

Back down under, wombats (one of Australia's pouched mammals) make square pwoos.

Poo is very important down on the farm. All cows eat grass, which is mainly made of **cellulose** (cell-you-lows). Cows cannot make the enzymes that turn cellulose into the sugars that give them energy. Instead, they have big grinding teeth and four stomachs.

The **reticulum** (ret-tick-you-lum) is the smallest stomach but has strong muscles trained in the art of throwing up. Cows are **ruminants**, which means they are sick on purpose so that they can chew their food again. This is called **chewing the cud**. No wonder cows burp a lot!

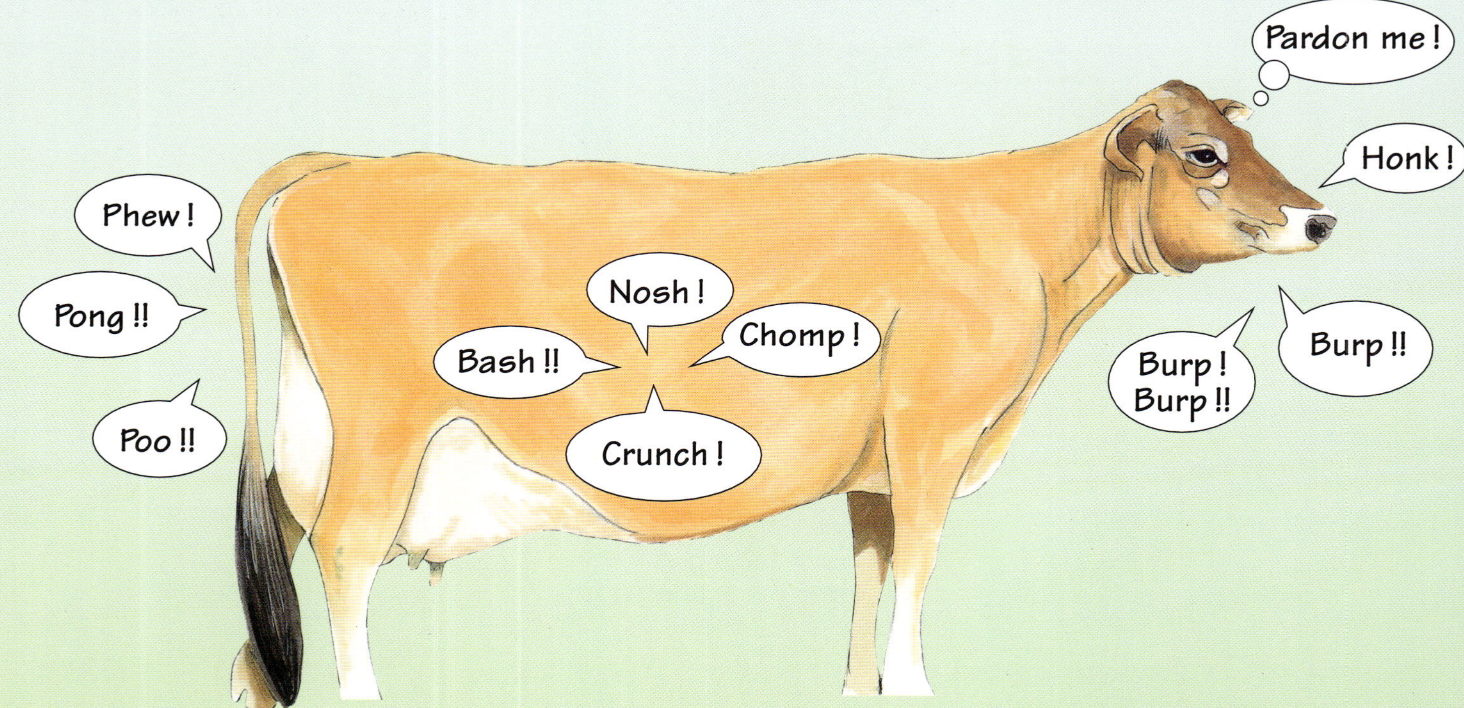

There is lots of room in the biggest stomach, which is called the **rumen**. Here, well-chewed food is mixed with bacteria, yeast and mini-beasts called **protists**. Many of these can smash up cellulose in the cow's stomach.

The **omasum** (oh-mass-um) and **abomasum** are stomachs full of food mixed with those tiny bacteria that turn cellulose into sweet sugar. Lots more gas is produced, including methane.

Cows make pancake poos called pats or claps (or zigzags if they are walking!).

Horses and sheep don't chew the cud and have only one stomach. Part of their intestine is a large, sac-like **caecum** (see-cum) in which friendly bacteria aid their digestive system.

Many people living in poor countries can't afford to buy wood, let alone electricity. They cook their food by burning sun-dried cow pats, 400 million tonnes (or 400 thousand million pats) a year in Asia and Africa alone. If this was used as organic fertilizer it would enrich the soil and help make 200 million tonnes more food.

We might grumble about exhaust fumes today, but think what town life would be like if there were no cars, only horses.

Piles of poo or pwoo in the wrong place cause problems.

There are now more chickens in the world than any other sort of bird. Sadly, most of them live in cramped conditions in battery cages. Although their pwoo is rich in plant food, like phosphate and nitrate, it can cause pollution.

Pigs are often reared on factory farms, and when their poo and wee mixes together it causes all sorts of trouble.

It pollutes the air with **ammonia**, and the soil, streams and rivers with a poisonous slurry with a high **BOD**.

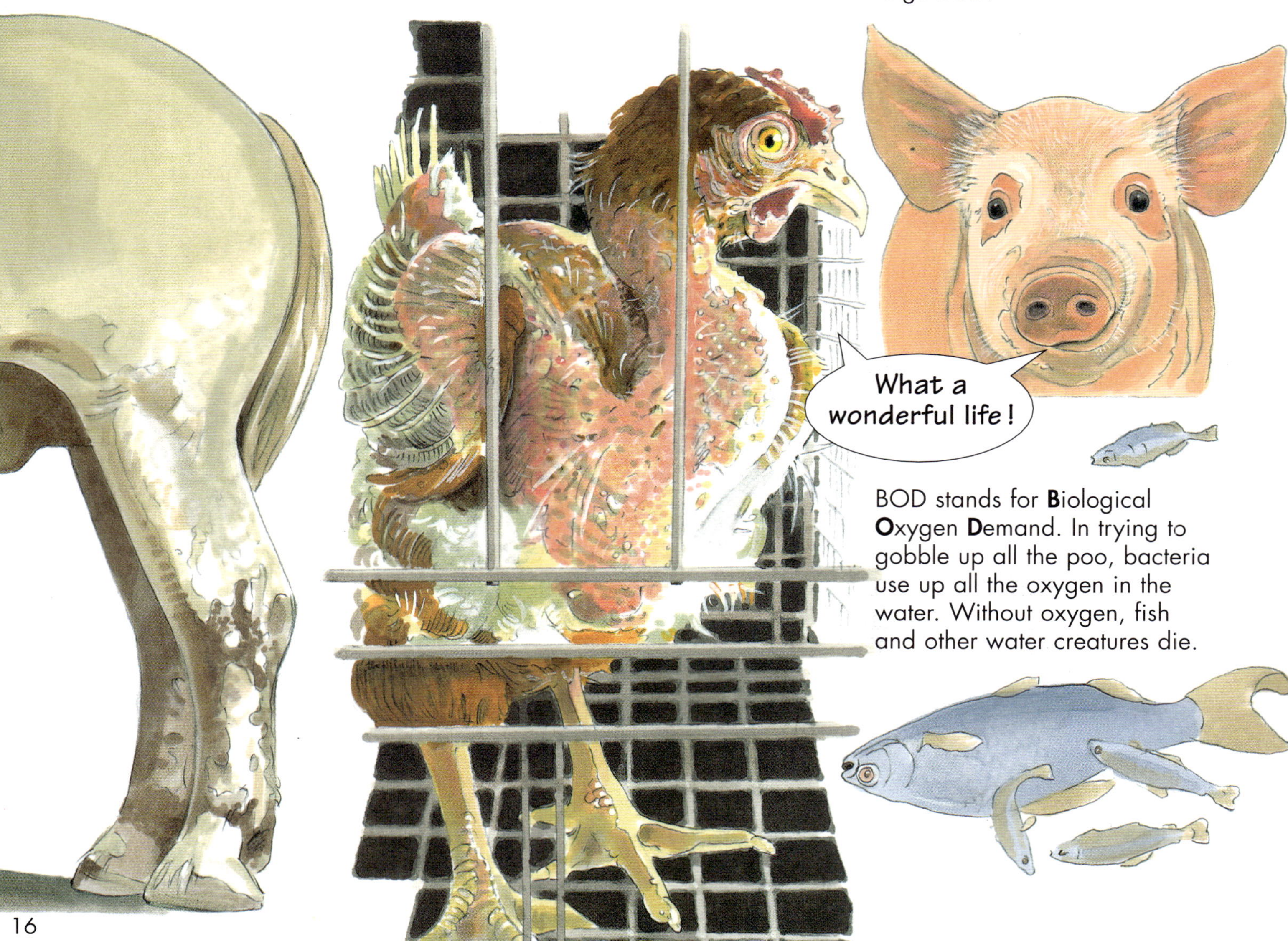

BOD stands for **B**iological **O**xygen **D**emand. In trying to gobble up all the poo, bacteria use up all the oxygen in the water. Without oxygen, fish and other water creatures die.

Let's go for a day in the country, away from all those people and the problems of poos.

The first is easy but the second impossible, for even in the deepest, darkest national park you are surrounded by the stuff.

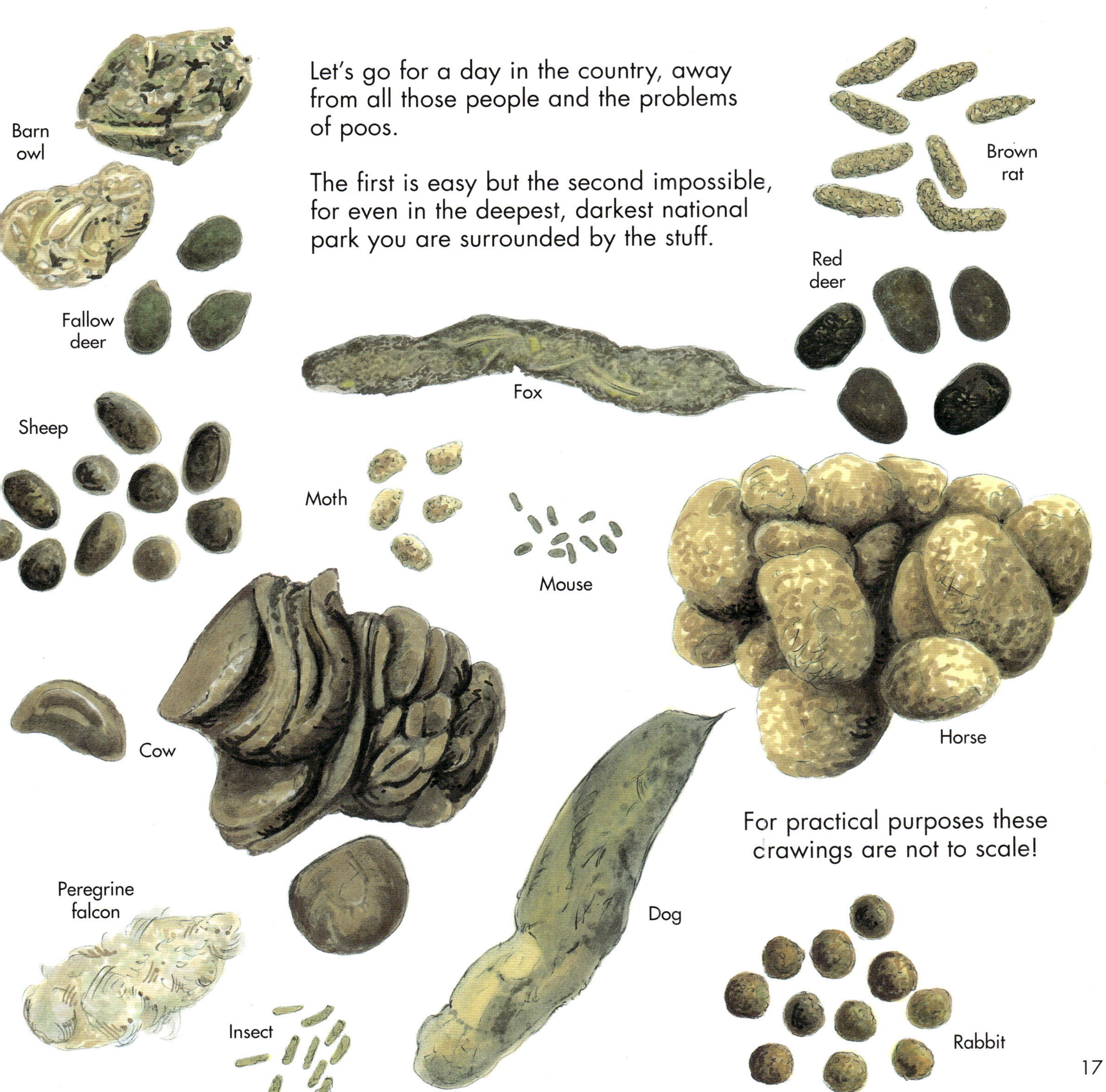

For practical purposes these drawings are not to scale!

Rabbits are prolific pooers with very strange habits. Vegetarian by nature, but not ruminants, they **refect**. That means they eat their fresh poo, giving their friendly bacteria another chance at cellulose bashing.

Badgers dig latrines at a convenient distance from their setts.

Owls have a real problem. Their food comes ready-wrapped in fur and full of bones. They get rid of waste at both ends: they regurgitate pellets at the top and pwoo at the bottom. Each pellet is a mini-museum, a menu of all they have eaten.

Foxes face the same problem with fortitude. Bony and furry bits pass right through them. Foxes climb trees and so do hedgehogs, in search of food. Squirrels too and they all poo, unyucky you!

Never fear, it is very unlikely that you would be pooed or pelleted from above. There is, however, one waste product that will always get you, the dreaded **frass**. Imagine the scene ... a woodland walk in the summer, bird song echoing through the trees, the gentle sound of bees humming...

...but, above your head, mega-legions of caterpillars are feeding on leaves. Billions of aphids, well stuck into the local sap supply, are leaking sticky honeydew from their rear ends. Add to this the marauding mobs of spiders, harvestmen and ants feeding on these vegetarian hoards, all chewing and pwooing, making frass.

Sit quietly on a still summer day and you can hear a gentle whisper of falling frass. So, all you have to do is wear a hat or think of it as pure organic hairspray!

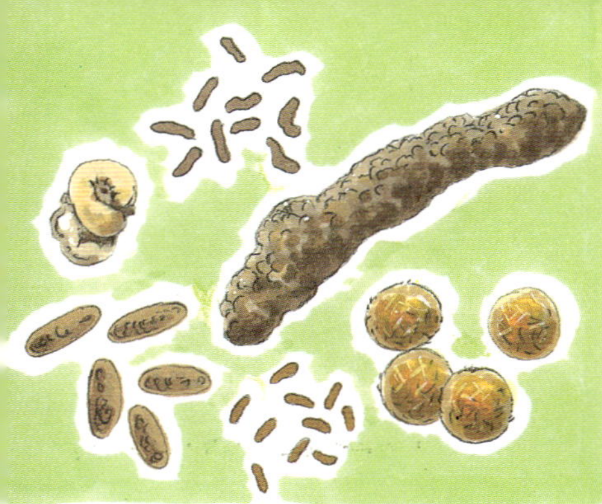

They may be waste to us but frass, pwoos and poos are made of organic matter, full of energy and nutrients. They make an ideal home for anything clever enough to eat what the animal has left behind. New poo of any sort is paradise for moulds, toadstools and bacteria.

A **mould** called *Pilobolus* (pie-low-bow-luss) moves in first. Humans have babies, moulds make **spores**. *Pilobolus* produce theirs in guns on the top of long stalks. Each stalk has a kind of 'eye' that guides it towards the light. This means it never shoots its spores down into the poo, but up on to the grass, ready to be eaten by another animal. The spores are so tough they pass right through the animal, to emerge ready potted. It may be poo to you but it is an intensive-care unit for a baby *Pilobolus*!

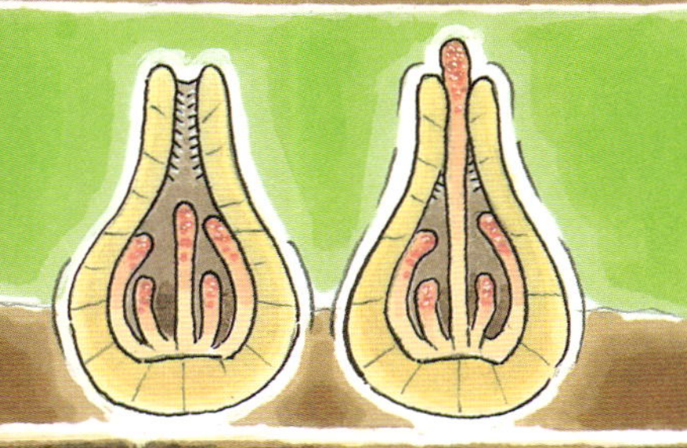

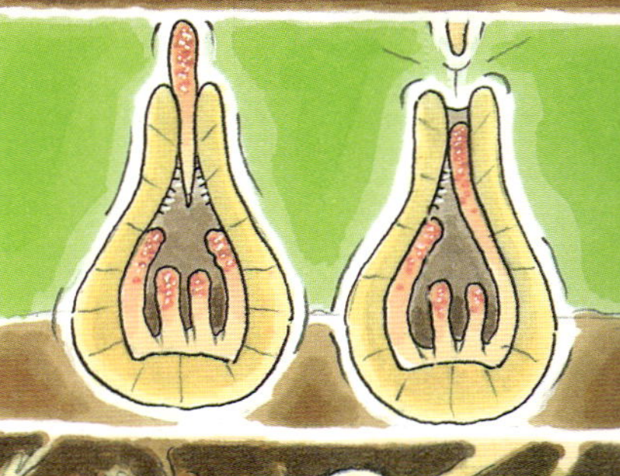

The flask fungi thrive on leftovers that the mould could not use. When they have used all they can, their spore guns poke out from inside a protective flask and launch their next generation of poo crunchers into the air.

Then come the toadstools, feeding on the vintage poo. Their spores fall from gills underneath the parasol.

Some mosses grow on old poo. Their spores stick to the feet of visiting flies and get carried from one poo to another.

Dung beetles collect poo and make it into large balls, which they roll into their burrows. There, out of sight, it feeds their babies.

The bulk of the poo is used up, the rest is broken down by hard-working bacteria, and recycled into the soil.

All these animals, fungi and bacteria are working together as nature's own garbage gang. They keep the countryside clean and tidy and the soil replenished with nutrients.

Every natural landscape deals with its own waste, feeding the worms and recycling the minerals. Microscopic creatures of wetlands and rivers are especially good at this. Under natural conditions they keep water pure and clear.

The sub-aqua garbage gang, especially the bacteria, do their best, but they may use up all the oxygen in the water. If that happens, only sewage fungus survives.

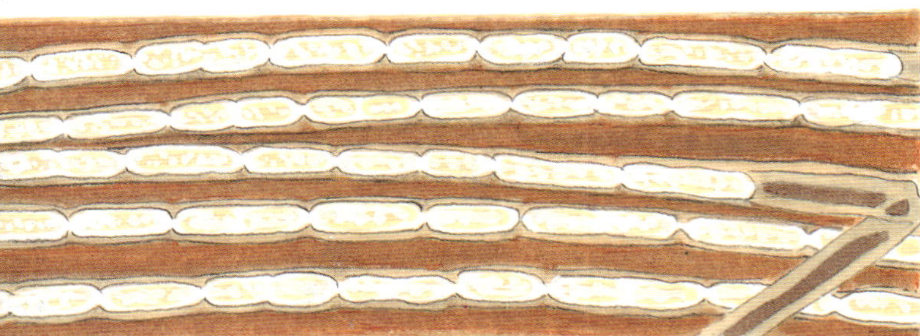

Frogs and swallows feast on the flies, while water tumbling over the weir stirs in oxygen, breathing life back into the river.

Unfortunately, people soon learned that rivers are nature's own free-flowing 'spooage' works and built their long drops over moats and rivers. With Thomas Crapper's invention, they soon flushed too much in. Plopville – what a mess!

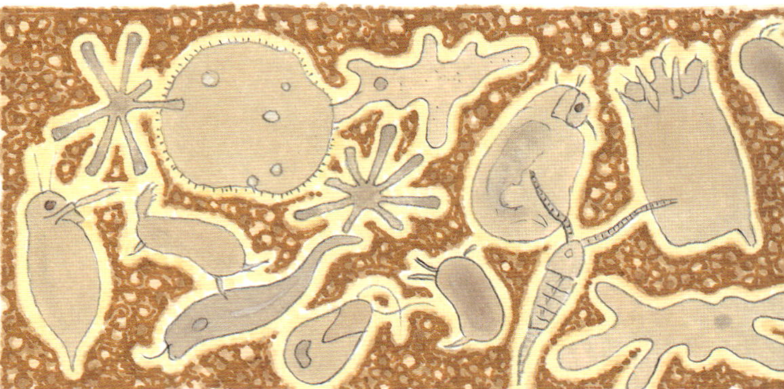

The water flows on, and further downstream the garbage gang begin to win the battle and start to clear up the problem.

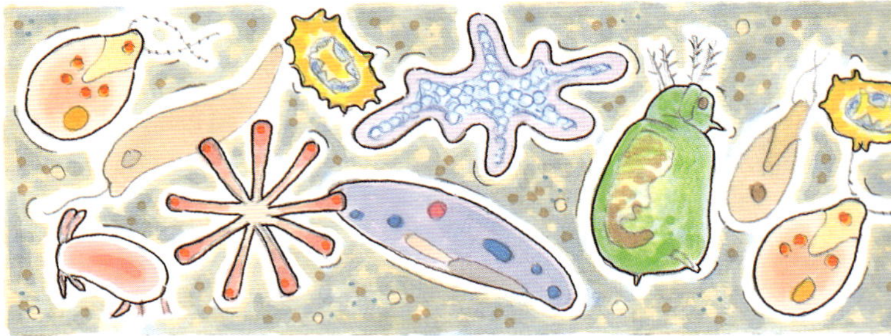

When water evaporates into the air to form clouds, it leaves the problems behind.

But water plants can now grow again, releasing lots more oxygen. Fish are thriving. The river is rich in nutrients.

These nutrients help to make plants grow, producing lots of food for ducks, swans and fish. Slowly the river comes back into balance.

Sadly, not for long...
...Pooalot is around the next meander.

No wonder rivers like the Thames had become a stinking mess by the end of the nineteenth century.

Something had to be done, and very soon sewage works were invented. London's first one was opened by Prince Albert with a banquet held in the settling tank (before it was filled!).

Today, sewage from millions of homes comes in via the main sewer pipe. First, all the rubbish is screened off. Who threw that pair of tights down the loo?

After settling, any solids can be used as fertilizer or as fuel to make electricity.

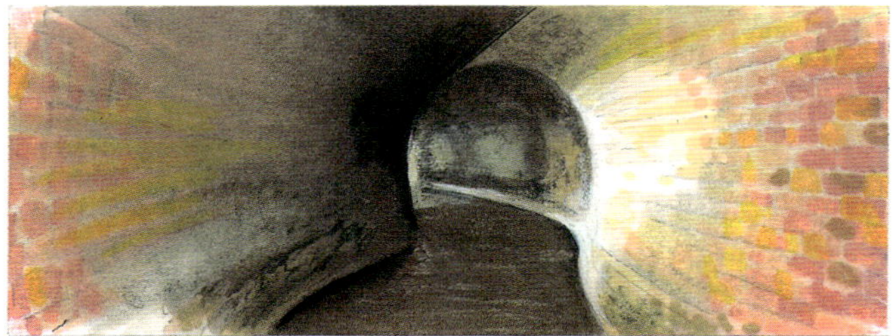

Then poo and water go into the **bio-digester**, a giant drum with paddles inside that really stirs things up. Bacteria love it there and smash up the poo as quickly as they can. This makes methane gas, which is used as energy to fuel the works.

The liquid, still rich in pulverized poo and nutrients, has a high BOD. Giant sprinklers spray this on to **filter beds** packed full of more bacteria that complete the job. The filters look like giant gramophone records (always playing Top of the Plops!).

After filtration, the water is pure and clear but out of balance. It has too many nutrients and is bung-full of bacteria, some of which can cause disease.

In the most up-to-date sewage works, ultraviolet light waves kill the bacteria and specially made wetlands use up the nutrients, growing, for instance, reeds for thatching.

The water is then returned to the river or the sea for nature to take its course.

Most of the tap water we drink comes from reservoirs or rivers, or from sources deep in porous rocks. Where necessary, it is filtered through beds of clean sand and treated with chemicals before it is ready to drink.

Until recently, most of our sewage sludge was dumped in the sea via rivers, pipes and special poo ships. New laws are changing this and our poo is now being put to better use. In Australia they have even given it another name, **biosolids**.

In the nineteenth century, sailors braved the stormy seas around Cape Horn to reach treasure islands off the coast of Peru. They returned to Europe, not with gold or gems, but with **guano** (gwar-no). Guano is sea bird pwoo, a rich fertilizer that collects on islands that have little rain to wash it away.

The people of Nauru, a tiny Pacific island, are among the richest in the world thanks to pwoo. For tens of thousands of years, sea birds have fished the rich waters and returned to perch, preen and pwoo on land. As a result, the surface rock is the richest source of phosphate fertilizer in the world. The islanders have invested the money they make and live off the pwofits of pwoo.

Penguin rookeries are noisy, smelly, pwooey places, and so are the shores where seals haul out to calve.

The blue whale may be the world's biggest pooer, but it depends on plankton, which are tiny plants and animals floating in the sea. It takes one thousand tonnes of plant plankton to feed one hundred tonnes of animal plankton, which feeds ten tonnes of whale. In the short months of the Antarctic summer, blue whales eat enough food to allow them to migrate to the other end of the Earth without feeding or pooing again.

Most of the animals of the open sea depend on plant plankton. Dead remains of plants and animals sink down and down, feeding the strange denizens of the deep. The toughest and most indigestible bits collect as pwooze which covers the deep-ocean floor. This contains the **carbon dioxide** originally locked up by the plant plankton in the sunlight zone high above. Once on the bottom, it may remain there for millions of years. Scientists believe that carbon dioxide pouring into our atmosphere from burning forests and fossil fuels is making our planet warmer. Pwooze helps keep this under control.

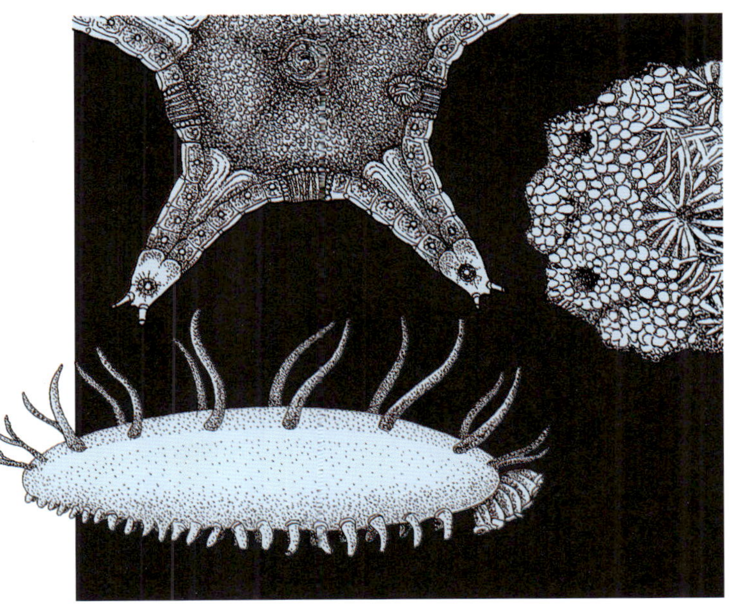

Poo in the right place works wonders; in the wrong place it makes an awful mess. Right now the world is in trouble and it can only get worse unless we learn the lesson of the potoroo's loo.

Poo is too precious to throw away. Recycle it to help trees, crops and flowers grow, so that they make oxygen and clean up the environment.

On land, one-third of all the world's productive soils are beginning to turn into deserts. They should never have been ploughed up and planted with crops. They should have been allowed to grow what they grow best, flower-filled grasslands for contented cows and sheep.

If farm animals were allowed to live more natural lives in diverse free-ranging farms, surrounded by forests and wetlands, the poo cycle could be put back into proper balance.

By the year 2035 humans and their farm animals could be producing about 16 billion tonnes of rich damp poo. That is enough to help produce millions more tonnes of food and put organic matter back into poor soil (or to flood the whole continent of Australia to a depth of over 40 centimetres!).

Already there are sewage works turning poo into odour-free granules to spread on fields. Granules from industrial towns are being used to help trees grow and stop the spread of deserts, and even to make bricks for building houses.

You can now buy your own electric loo that produces odour-free granules to fertilize your garden.

Then there are all those goodies like phosphates and nitrates in the waste water. At present these flow down into the sea and cause plankton called **dinoflagellates** (dye-no-flad-gel-lates) to multiply out of control. They turn the sea red and make shellfish like mussels and oysters poisonous for us to eat.

Phosphates and nitrates can be removed by inventions called **biocoils**. These are made of clear plastic tubing through which the waste water is passed. Mini-plants called *Chlorella* (claw-rella) live in these tubes, soaking up all the phosphate and nitrate and producing more *Chlorella*. Dried *Chlorella* can be fed to animals or used as slow-release organic fertilizer. They are also an excellent substitute for diesel fuel.

You can even run your car on poo. Like the people of Nauru you could become a poo millionaire, at the same time helping to put the world back into proper working order.

Now wash your hands.